FIDEL CASTRO

Richard Platt

RAINTREE
STECK-VAUGHN
PUBLISHERS

A Harcourt Company

Austin   New York
www.raintreesteckvaughn.com

Copyright Permissions
Steck-Vaughn Company
P.O. Box 26015
Austin, TX 78755

Published by Raintree Steck-Vaughn Publishers, an imprint of Steck-Vaughn Company

Library of Congress Cataloging-in-Publication Data

Cataloging-in-publication data is available at the Library of Congress.

ISBN 0-7398-6141-7

Printed in Hong Kong/China. Bound in the United States.

1 2 3 4 5 6 7 8 9 0 LB 05 04 03 02

Picture credits
Front cover: Popperfoto/Rafael Perez/Reuters (main picture); Topham Picturepoint (background)
Back cover: Popperfoto/Rafael Perez/Reuters

Frank Spooner Pictures/Gamma pp. 11, 14, 17
Peter Newark's American Pictures pp. 9, 33, 37, 43, 75, 85, 92
Popperfoto pp. 2, 3 (Rafael Perez/Reuters), 5 (Eric Miller/Reuters), 21, 27, 28, 30, 39, 40, 48, 52, 59, 67, 69, 71 (Rafael Perez/Reuters), 73, 76, 78, 81, 83, 91, 98 (Rafael Perez/Reuters), 101 (Diario Granma/Reuters), 102 (Adalberto Roque/AFP), 105 (Rafael Perez/Reuters)
South American Pictures/Tony Morrison pp. 13, 23, 25
Topham Picturepoint pp. 7, 19 (Associated Press), 29, 44, 47 (Associated Press), 51, 55, 56, 61, 63, 65, 72, 79, 86, 89, 94 (Associated Press), 97 (Associated Press)

Fidel Castro
1926–

Contents

Introduction

Just 90 miles (150 km) of sea separate Cuba, the biggest island in the Caribbean, from Florida, mainland America's most southern state. You can sail across in just a few hours, but the two places could not be more different.

Nicknamed "The Sunshine State," Florida is best known for vacations, retirement homes, and Walt Disney World. Cuba is famous for sugar, cigars, and communism.

Cuban people each have about $1,500 a year to buy everything they need. On average, people in Florida spend this amount every 19 days.

As part of the United States, Florida holds regular elections in which everyone votes to choose who will make state and national laws. Cuba holds elections, too, but voters don't have much of a choice. For there is only one political party in Cuba: the Cuban Communist Party. Its leader, Fidel Castro, rules the only communist nation in the western half of the world. He has governed Cuba, more or less on his own, for more than 40 years.

This book is Fidel Castro's story. As you turn the pages, you'll find out how the son of a wealthy Cuban sugar farmer became a lawyer and politician. You'll read how he fled to Mexico, and gathered weapons and comrades to start a rebellion against Cuba's government. And you'll discover how, despite blunders and setbacks, and against powerful opposition, Castro's revolution eventually succeeded.

Castro continues to voice strong political views. He is shown here criticizing the United Nations for being unrepresentative and a front for a "new colonialism."

Old Cuba

Castro began his fight against Cuba's rulers because they were greedy and corrupt, and did not treat Cuba's people fairly.

Unfairness was nothing new to Cuba: the island had a history of injustice stretching back to the time, 500 years ago, when it was first discovered by Spanish explorers. The Spaniards claimed the island for Spain and took the land of the native people as their own. In the 1700s descendants of those Spanish settlers began to farm sugar cane, using slaves brought from Africa in conditions of great cruelty.

Cuba's Spanish rulers were corrupt, inefficient, and unpopular. A feeling of injustice built up until, in 1868, Cubans began fighting the Spanish for independence (the right to govern themselves, free of Spanish control). The war lasted ten years and achieved almost nothing.

In the years that followed, the influence of the United States grew in Cuba. American companies bought greater amounts of sugar and other goods, and Cuban ports bustled with ships bringing American imported goods. U.S. firms bought up land and opened offices in the capital, Havana.

When the independence movement flared up again at the end of the 19th century, Cubans now had a powerful ally in their fight with Spain. With help from the United States, Cubans at last won their independence in 1899, but there was a price to pay. The Americans did not want Cuba ruled by revolutionaries, so when the war of independence ended, U.S. troops stayed on. They helped to make the island safe and repaired the damage war had caused. But they also made sure that any new government would respect the United States, its people, and its businesses.

Before the Americans left in 1902, they guided the Cubans in the creation of a new constitution (rules of government). Although this prepared Cuba for fair elections, it also gave the United States

▶ *Shown here is a street in Havana, the capital of Cuba, in 1926, the year Fidel Castro was born.*

the right to rule Cuba directly if the country ever became a danger to its much bigger neighbor.

Independence and elections

Cubans voted for the first time in 1901, but the elections did not bring them the justice and fairness they had hoped for. Instead of governing wisely, the politicians looked for ways to increase their power and make themselves rich. For the first half of the 20th century, most of Cuba's rulers were corrupt. They took bribes and cheated at elections to make sure that they would win again and again. For example, Tomás Estrada Palma, Cuba's first president, rigged elections to Congress. His supporters made sure that he could not lose the presidential elections in 1905. Mario Menocal, elected in 1912 and again in 1916, was wealthy when he took office, but was an astonishing $40 million richer after eight years as president.

Cuban people who were outside the golden circle of rich politicians and their friends had a very hard time indeed. Most country people were extremely poor. Few owned their own farms; three-quarters of Cuba's land belonged to foreigners. Afro-Cubans, the descendants of the sugar-farm slaves, faced special hardships, because racial prejudice kept them in the worst jobs and homes.

Cuba's social injustice and corrupt governments angered Fidel Castro. He believed it was his mission to lead his people to a better, fairer future in which everyone had the same opportunities. How he set out to achieve this aim is an astonishing story of luck, stubbornness, and wild ambition.

King Sugar

The sweet taste of sugar made Cuba rich in the 1800s, and poor in the 20th century. By 1860 slaves in Cuba were growing a third of all the world's sugar and high prices meant that the island flourished.

But as other countries started to grow sugar, prices fell. Prices could change very quickly, too: the value of a crop often doubled or halved from one year to the next. Even in a good year, sugar workers suffered, because they had jobs for only a few months during the harvest season. At other times, they were unemployed.

▶ *Advertising posters encouraged wealthy Americans to come to Cuba for their vacations. Most Cuban people gained little from tourism.*

GAY DAYS UNDER THE CUBAN SUN

Hotel Nacional de Cuba
HAVANA

Right on the shore in Havana, the Nacional stands
in 13 acres of flowering gardens. Two swimming pools,
tennis and many other forms of recreation offer the
winter vacationist the ultimate in luxury.

A Kirkeby Hotel

A corner of the
new Cabana Sun Club . . .
daily rendezvous of the
smart cosmopolitan set who
revel in Cuba's unfailing sunshine

Schoolboy and Student

A single gunshot rang out across the village of Birán, in Cuba's most eastern province, Oriente. Instantly, the children playing in a nearby field dropped their game and ran home. Fidel Castro led the charge.

Besides being the fittest, Fidel was also the hungriest of them. The echoing shotgun blast was just their mother's signal that dinner was ready!

The house they crowded into was a strange, messy collection of wooden rooms on stilts. Chickens and turkeys scratched in the shade beneath. Not far away there was a large barn, a repair shop, and a slaughterhouse. Looking at the ramshackle place, only the size hinted that Fidel's father, Angel, was the wealthiest farmer in the area. He employed hundreds of peasant workers to grow and cut sugar cane.

There was the usual crowd for dinner. Servants and visitors ate with the family, and there were many children to feed. Pedro Emilio and Lidia were the oldest. When their mother had died, soon after Lidia was born, Fidel's father had married the family maid, Lina. Fidel was their fourth child together, after Ángela, Agustina, and Ramón. Fidel also had a younger brother Raúl, and later two more sisters, Enma and Juana, would swell the family further.

Classroom troublemaker

Family dinners and games in the cane fields ended when Fidel reached the age of four and was packed off to a local school. He did not like the change. At home he could do more or less what he liked. At school he was supposed to sit still, study, and obey his teachers. He didn't. Instead, he caused trouble.

▶ *Fidel is dressed in his best clothes at the age of three. These were the carefree days of childhood.*

Within a year, the school and his parents had had enough. They sent Fidel to live with his godparents in Santiago, Cuba's second largest city. At a private school there, priests taught Fidel.

Fidel didn't like his second school any better than the first, even when two of his brothers joined him in classes. Fidel argued with his teachers. He fought other students. He saw school as a jail and longed for the vacations. When the school told his father that the Castro boys were "the three biggest bullies" in the school, all three were brought home, to Fidel's delight.

His joy did not last long. When school began again, his father sent him to an *even stricter* church school, again in Santiago. There, Fidel at last found something he was good at: sports. He was strong and fit and made the boxing, soccer, and baseball teams. In his classes though, he did as little as he could get away with, scraping through his exams by last-minute cramming.

At sixteen, Fidel changed schools again —this time moving to the island's capital, Havana. And once more, it was his ability in sports that gave him an advantage. In his classes he did well in subjects that interested him—farming, history, geography, and Spanish, the language of Cuba. But in other subjects, he worked just hard enough to graduate, and in 1945 he won a place at the law school of Havana University.

Fidel studies revolution

In 1945 Havana University was an exciting and dangerous place. Cuba's political parties all had student members, and within the university grounds political arguments were often settled with fights or shootings. The victors in these gang battles hoped to gain more power not just in the university, but everywhere in the country. Just as politics was an important part of student life, students played an important part in Cuban politics.

There was also money at stake: student gangsters controlled the sale of textbooks and could fix grades by threatening professors. Fidel may have been enrolled in a law course, but he ended up joining a school for revolutionary politics.

Fidel loved the excitement and danger, and many of the people he knew were members of two of the most important gangs: the Socialist Revolutionary

Movement (MSR) and the Insurrectional Revolutionary Union (UIR). The MSR was an anti-communist revolutionary socialist party which fought the influence of the United States. The rival UIR seemed to have few policies except the elimation of its opponents. At first Fidel avoided getting too closely involved with these "action groups." He realized that by joining either, he would gain many enemies and win few friends.

After just a year at the university, Fidel had already learned some vital political skills. His speech at a university festival was such a well-composed attack on Cuba's corrupt government that it made front-page news in the island's papers.

▼ Fidel's family farm was in eastern Cuba, in a landscape similar to this. Their house was also a low wooden structure, but bigger than this one.

Politics was sucking Fidel in: when anti-government politicians formed a new group, the Cuban People's Party, he joined. In angry writings, he criticized Cuba's rulers and the violent gangsters. But his enthusiasm for politics did not stop at speeches and articles. Fidel was hungry for action, and soon he tasted it.

Toppling dictators

To the east of Cuba lies the Caribbean's second-biggest island. The Dominican Republic, at the eastern end of this nearby island, was a dictatorship. The country's president kept all political power for himself and ruthlessly crushed opposition. Dominican people living in

Cuba planned to sail home and liberate their country from the dictator's grip. In spite of his father's pleas and his mother's tears, Fidel joined them in the summer of 1947 and began training as a revolutionary fighter in a remote area of Cuba. By mid-September the 1,200-strong amateur army was ready.

They never reached their destination. Before they had even sailed out of sight of land, the Cuban navy stopped the revolutionaries' four cargo ships and arrested everybody they could find. Fidel escaped and swam to shore.

Six months later, he saw for the first time the power of ordinary, angry people. He had flown to Bogotá, Colombia's capital, for a student conference. While he was there, gunmen shot and killed a political leader who was a hero among the country's poorest people. Riots began as soon as news of the assassination spread. Fidel watched in amazement from the balcony of his hotel. Mobs of rioters were overturning cars, taking over the radio station, and invading government buildings. He went down and mingled with them as they stormed a police station and stole guns. The excitement was electrifying, but the danger was obvious, too, so he wisely slipped back to Cuba.

Law school studies

Fidel spent the next two years much as he had spent the previous three. He built a reputation as a fierce and reckless opponent of the government—and neglected his law studies. When exam time came, he had to make a superhuman effort to pass. For the spring and summer of 1950, he dropped politics completely, burying himself in university work. His intensive studies paid off, and in September, he graduated and opened a law office with two fellow students in Havana's business district.

Fidel's studying and political work left him little time for play. He was shy with women, and unlike most of his fellow students, he never went dancing in Havana's many nightclubs. Nevertheless, when he met philosophy student Mirta Díaz-Balart, Fidel was enchanted. They married in the fall of 1948, and had a son, Fidelito, a year later.

◀ *Ángela, Ramón, and Fidel (aged eight) pose for a photo in 1934. At this time, Fidel was going to a private school in Santiago.*

Lawyer and Rebel Leader

Fidel Castro was no ordinary lawyer. Unlike many lawyers, he was not interested in making money. His only clients were poor peasants and city slum dwellers. He rarely got paid, and when he did, he was more likely to be given fruit and vegetables than cash.

Castro did not look like a lawyer, either. He did not wear a neatly-pressed suit. He looked as if he had slept in his clothes. Often he had.

His personal life was in chaos. His father had given him a brand-new car as a college graduation present, but he lent it to a friend who smashed it beyond repair. The electricity in his apartment was cut off because the bill wasn't paid. Debt collectors took away his furniture, and he paid as little attention to his wife and son as he did to his bank account.

Castro cared about only one thing: politics. He even used his law practice to advance his political career. By pleading the hopeless cases of Cuba's poor, he believed he could get a reputation as a champion of the people.

Dangerous ideas

It was a fine idea, but Castro faced many obstacles. His political opinions were very extreme, and his methods put him in great personal danger. He openly accused politicians of corruption and produced evidence that they had taken bribes. This made him a target for the political gangsters who supported his opponents. To protect himself, Castro never went anywhere without a revolver, and he did not hesitate to use it.

Castro's views were so extreme that he began to lose support even within his own party, now nicknamed the "Orthodoxo" party. He had wanted to run

▶ Castro's gift for impassioned speech-making served him well as a lawyer and later as a political leader.

for the Cuban Congress in the 1952 elections but Roberto Agramonte, the Orthodoxo's presidential candidate, made sure that Castro's name was not on the list of official candidates.

It took more than a trick like this to stop Castro. He visited Havana's poorest district, La Pelusa, where he led opponents of a government plan to tear down the neighborhood and build a grand square. Castro had helped the slum dwellers by holding rallies where he explained how they could fight for their rights. He also won 50 pesos compensation for each home affected. These campaigns made him a local hero, and he had no difficulty getting the people of the slums to nominate him as an Orthodoxo candidate.

The campaign trail

Castro's election campaign was spectacular and original. He used a regular spot on a radio program to spread his message. Besides making speeches and writing pamphlets, Castro sent individual letters to all the Orthodoxo supporters in the region—100,000 of them. Mail campaigns like this are common in today's elections, but in 1950s Cuba they were unheard of.

He might as well not have bothered, because Cubans never got the chance to cast their votes. On March 10, 1952, two months before the elections were due, there was a military *coup* (a sudden, illegal change of power). Cuba's retired president, Fulgencio Batista, took control of the country with the help of the Cuban army. There was no opposition: in fact many Cubans were delighted. They hoped Batista would end corruption and control the armed gangs who were making everyday life dangerous. But Batista began to rule Cuba as a dictator, throwing opponents in prison and disbanding political parties. He also stole enormous sums of public money.

Conditions in Cuba improved at first. As he had promised, Batista cracked down on the gangsters. By doing deals with the labor unions, the dictator stopped strikes that had been harming the country's businesses. But within a year, these advantages began to seem less important to many Cuban people than the political rights that Batista had taken away from them.

▶ *The Batista family lived extremely comfortably on their estate outside Havana, benefiting from the corrupt dictatorship of the father, Fulgencio Batista.*

"Down with Batista!"

Opposition to the dictator grew. Directly after the coup, Castro had found little support for his violent aim of forcing Batista from power. But as time went by, more and more people joined the underground revolutionary movement he was building.

They were not just attracted by Castro's aims. It was his personality and character that excited his followers. Castro had charisma—the ability to capture people's imagination, and make them believe anything was possible. His appearance helped, too: at more than six feet tall, and heavily built, he almost glowed with power.

Castro knew he had to be very wary and careful: Batista had spies everywhere. For example, when he heard of the coup, Castro guessed (correctly, as it turned out) that the secret police would come to arrest him. He left the tiny apartment where he was living with his wife and son, and went to stay with his sister Lidia, about a mile away. From there he moved to the safety of the houses of sympathizers of the rebel movement, including the luxury home of Naty Revuelta. Intelligent, wealthy, and beautiful, Naty was drawn to Castro's idealistic politics, but she also found him very attractive: they later fell in love, and had a daughter, Alina together.

Moving regularly from house to house in Havana, Castro gathered around him a small group of people he could trust. Together they laid plans for a daring guerrilla attack on government forces.

All agreed that without weapons they could do nothing, so they hatched a secret plot to steal guns and ammunition from the Cuban army. In the city of Santiago, a 15-hour drive away from Havana, Moncada Barracks (an army base) had huge stores of arms. If they could attack the barracks, there would be enough guns for everyone.

Hitting the barracks

The plotters worked in great secrecy. Castro sent a spy to Santiago and he returned with a sketched map of Moncada. An army officer who opposed the government gave them a hundred uniforms. A member of the group rented a nearby house and bought a few rifles.

▶ *Fulgencio Batista inspects a U.S. tank, a gift of military aid from the U.S. government which supported his regime.*

On July 26, 1953 everything was ready. The 200 revolutionaries set off for the barracks in cars. At the guard house to the barracks one of them shouted, "Let the general in!" The simple trick worked. Instead of checking the suspicious car, the guards sprang to attention. Instantly, the other revolutionaries jumped out and knocked them to the ground.

But the carefully laid plan started to go wrong when other sentries raised the alarm. Firing wildly, Castro's men rushed to where their maps showed the armory (weapons store) to be. When they got there, they found a barbershop! There was worse to come—most of Castro's fighters got lost in Santiago's streets. The daring attack suddenly looked badly planned. Eight of the attackers lay dead; many more were injured. Within a day or so, the army rounded up most of the rest.

Rounding up the rebels

Five days after the attack, an army patrol found Castro fast asleep on the floor of a peasant's shack and arrested him. He was put on trial in Santiago along with about a hundred of his followers. When the trial began, Castro spoke in his own defense. Whenever he was asked a question, he turned his reply into an attack on the government. His proud speeches embarrassed the judge, and Castro did not appear in public court again. His trial was held later in secret, and he was given a 15-year prison sentence.

While in prison, Castro was shocked to learn that his wife, Mirta, had been fired from a job at the Interior Ministry. He had not even realized she had been employed by the Batista government, and he felt bitter and betrayed. He immediately began divorce proceedings. Later, when the split was complete, Mirta married again, and moved to the U.S.

However, this personal tragedy was overshadowed by a political project. Castro was writing a long revolutionary statement called *History Will Absolve Me*. The title was a phrase Castro used to defend himself at his trial. He meant that in future years, everybody would see that he was not guilty.

Spreading the word

In *History Will Absolve Me*, Castro set out his plans for Cuba. These included giving people back their political freedoms, giving land to the people who farmed it, allowing workers to share company profits, and seizing the property of corrupt politicians.

These were dangerous ideas, and Castro had to smuggle his writings out of the prison. The booklet was eventually printed and distributed by Castro's sister Lidia and two women revolutionaries who had avoided prison: Melba Hernandez and Haydé Santamaria.

▼ The Moncada Barracks in Santiago, scene of Castro's chaotic defeat, is now a museum to the July 26th Movement.

Guerrilla warfare

Castro planned to defeat Cuba's dictator with a *guerrilla war*—making small-scale attacks, constantly changing bases, and using sabotage and terrorism. By avoiding formal battles wherever possible, and by making surprise attacks, guerrilla fighters are able to defeat much larger armies of regular troops. However, fighting a successful guerrilla war demands exceptional leadership, support from the local people, and troops who are totally dedicated to victory.

Rebels in Waiting

The revolutionaries convicted for the Moncada attack spent less than two years in prison. As soon as the jail gates slammed behind them, a campaign for their release began. At the beginning of May 1955, Batista's government bowed to public pressure, and the prisoners were pardoned.

Castro was released from prison in a blaze of publicity. He was greeted by Melba, Haydé, his sister Lidia, and Naty Revuelta. Newspaper photographs show him in a crowd of admiring women. But when the excitement died down, he found himself on the fringes of Cuban politics. Even before the coup, he was too extreme and unpredictable to be selected as an Orthodoxo election candidate. With a dictator in power, the party considered him even more dangerous. This did not worry Castro. From Lidia's apartment where he was staying, he continued with his attacks on Batista just as he had before the suicidal attack on the barracks.

Castro may have been the most famous opponent of the government, but he was not the only one. Other groups were more violent, planting bombs and shooting Batista's agents. Eventually, the dictator became impatient of this terrorist activity and stopped pretending he was a moderate ruler. Cuba's short period of freedom ended: newspapers were censored or closed down, and the secret police rounded up, beat up, or simply killed anyone they suspected of plotting against the government.

One-way ticket to Mexico

Castro's movement was in serious danger. The leader began a wandering lifestyle, moving from one safe house to another, and never sleeping in the same place for more than one night. Castro's brother Raúl was accused of blowing up a movie theater. The charge was invented—

▶ This is the front cover of Fidel Castro's book, History Will Absolve Me, *written while he was imprisoned after the Moncada Barracks defeat.*

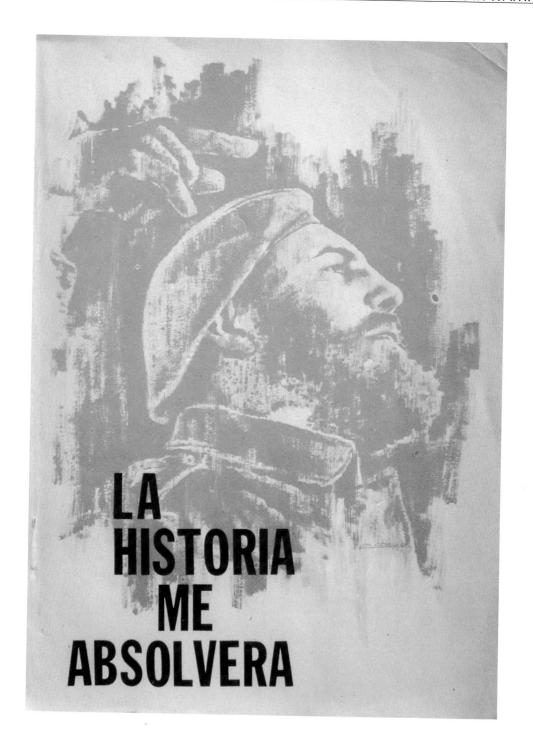

Batista's agents probably planted the bomb themselves—but it was clear that Havana was getting too hot for the rebels. In mid-summer, Raúl fled to the safety of Mexico. Castro followed him two weeks later; his sister Lidia sold her refrigerator to pay for the trip.

In Mexico Castro could carry on the fight without immediate danger. He quickly made himself at home in the capital, Mexico City, living in a cheap hotel and eating meals with friends. Although it was possible to live very cheaply—anyone with eight cents a day to spend would not starve—Castro was still penniless. Most of the money sent by supporters was spent on the rebel movement. To pay for the printing of a pamphlet, he took his overcoat to a pawn shop, and left it as security for a loan.

The one-eyed soldier

From his Mexico base, Castro bombarded his supporters in Cuba with revolutionary messages and continued his attacks on Batista. He also began serious planning for the armed invasion that he was convinced would start a revolution. He recognized that the Moncada Barracks attack had failed because he knew

nothing about warfare, so he looked for someone to help him train his invasion forces. He chose Alberto Byo, a one-eyed, Cuban-born soldier who had taught guerrilla warfare to the Spanish army. The white-haired old man was flattered, but amused—Castro had no money, no weapons, and no soldiers to train. However, he was charmed and impressed by the big Cuban, and agreed.

Castro and his friend Che Guevara formed the core of the new revolutionary group. It was now named the July 26th Movement after the date of the attack on the Moncada Barracks. The movement grew gradually in strength, as supporters arrived from Cuba. Most of these recruits had left their homeland to escape persecution by the muscular and well-armed "security police" that Batista employed to eliminate or terrify his opponents.

Castro would soon have all the rebels he needed, but he lacked money and guns. With one, he could buy the other, so he set off on a fund-raising tour of the United States. He did not expect any

▶ *New York City in the 1950s—one of the places Castro visited on his highly successful fund-raising tour of the United States.*

support from American people, who were generally happy with Cuba's dictator. But there were many Cubans living in the U.S. They had been emigrating to the U.S. since the late 1800s, and many had left in the 1950s to escape the country's economic problems. There was a large Cuban community of workers and businessmen in New York, and Cuban cigar workers had found jobs and settled in Tampa, Florida. These people filled Castro's meetings, and emptied their pockets of dollar bills at the end.

Castro promises freedom

In his speeches to packed halls, Castro made a promise: "I can inform you with complete certainty that in 1956 we will be free . . . !" With these words, he set himself a deadline: he would lead an invasion of Cuba within 14 months.

Soon after his return to Mexico, Castro was joyfully reunited with his son. Fidelito flew from Havana with Lidia, and during the remaining time in Mexico, Castro saw the boy whenever his revolutionary preparations allowed.

This wasn't as often as he would have liked, for, as usual, training and planning pushed almost everything else from Castro's mind. The small rebel army learned to shoot on a city rifle range. They marched and exercised to improve their stamina; they climbed mountains and slept on the bare ground so that they could endure the hardship of a guerrilla campaign. By spring 1956 they had outgrown their network of houses in the city, so Castro moved them to a walled ranch where they could train out of sight of curious onlookers—and Batista's spies.

Castro took enormous care to keep his activities in Mexico quiet, but at the same time he needed to drum up support for the movement back in Cuba. This made secrecy impossible, and Batista's secret police had no trouble rounding up members of the July 26th Movement in Havana. Batista's power did not stop at Cuba's shores. He paid assassins $20,000 to kidnap and murder Castro in Mexico.

◀ *While in Mexico City, Castro posed for this photograph taken in front of a partly finished symbol of his July 26th Movement.*

▶ *Che Guevara (in photo) was the ideal partner for Fidel Castro in the struggle to overthrow Cuba's dictator.*

Ernesto "Che" Guevara

In Mexico, Castro met other revolutionaries who shared his reasons for fleeing their home country. His most important contact was Argentine medical-school graduate Ernesto Guevara.

Ernesto—later nicknamed "Che"—had heard of Castro, and was impressed when they met. The two became close friends and remained so until shortly before Che's death. Their personalities matched perfectly. Che was a brilliant planner and thinker, but preferred to stay in the background. Castro was a born leader, a brilliant speaker, and an overpowering character, but lacked Che's political genius.

When the plan was discovered, the dictator looked for other ways to eliminate his irritating opponent.

Back in jail

On June 20 Mexico City police arrested Castro in the street and imprisoned him along with many other members of his group. Later they swooped down on the ranch, but not before the rebels had shipped out the store of guns and ammunition they had been collecting there. Castro was accused of planning Batista's assassination and of being a communist. He denied both charges, and it was true that he had no links with Cuba's Communist Party. If anything, the Cuban communists were rivals, rather than allies of the July 26th Movement.

After pressure from respected Mexican politicians, most of the rebels were released within three weeks. The charge against Castro was reduced to staying in Mexico after the visitor's permit on his passport had expired, and a week later he too was released. Che and one other rebel were kept behind bars until the end of July.

Free once more, they returned to their invasion plans. Even news of the death of his father in October barely distracted Castro from his urgent mission. Being arrested and imprisoned had taught him a valuable lesson—Batista's influence reached even to Mexico. They were no longer safe anywhere. In any case Castro had promised he would free his country in 1956. The revolution could wait no longer.

◄ *Shown is an aerial view of Mexico City from the mid-1950s. At first this seemed a safe place for Castro to plan his revolution but he soon realized that Batista's power reached into Mexico.*

Che and Fidel Fight for Freedom

"Where is the mother ship? When do we get to the real ship?" One of Castro's rebels simply could not believe his eyes as he boarded the *Granma*. Surely Castro could not launch his revolution from a 43-foot (13 meters) motor yacht? But that is exactly what he intended to do. This *was* the mother ship.

Castro had spent $20,000 on a patrol torpedo boat in Miami, but the American government, which was sympathetic to Batista, refused to let it sail. Castro's second choice, the *Granma*, was far less suitable. It was a pleasure boat designed to carry 12 passengers, not a crowd of 24.

Castro and his revolutionaries set off from the coast of Mexico. In rain-swept Tuxpan harbor, 81 revolutionaries clambered on board the *Granma* and loaded their guns and supplies. Fifty more were left behind, for fear the ship would sink. Finally, at 1:30 on the morning of Sunday November 25, 1956, the *Granma* cast off from her moorings, and sailed uncertainly down the Tuxpan River.

Sea-sick comrades

When they reached the sea, the commandos sang the Cuban national anthem. Some shouted "¡Viva la revolución!" and "Down with Batista's dictatorship!" Their joy did not last long. When the ship left the shelter of the river estuary, it took the full force of the storm that was swirling across the Gulf of Mexico. Within minutes, many of the rebels were violently ill. Overloaded, the *Granma* wallowed in the swell, and her badly-maintained diesel engines struggled against the tearing wind.

Castro had estimated that the crossing would take five days. So before leaving,

▶ *Raúl, Castro's younger brother (on the right), also became a revolutionary and took part in the 1956 attempted coup. He is pictured here with Che Guevara.*

he had sent coded messages to supporters in Cuba, telling them the revolution would start on Friday morning. By dawn on Friday, the *Granma* had completed only three-quarters of her voyage. The bad weather had slowed progress, and one of the engines was failing. The ship could cruise at only seven knots, instead of the ten that the plan called for. Without a radio transmitter, Castro had no way to warn his comrades on land that he was running late. So at 7 A.M. on Friday the revolution started—without its leader, and without the promised invasion.

In Santiago 28 rebels attacked the police headquarters, and set fire to the police barracks. But they were no match for the 400 specialist anti-guerrilla troops stationed in the town. After a day of street fighting, the Santiago rebellion collapsed.

Almost everywhere else on the island, anti-Batista groups were too weak to take up arms. Not *quite* everywhere, though. On a beach near Bélic, 24 revolutionaries scanned the horizon for a sight of the *Granma*. They waited . . . and waited. By Saturday morning Castro had still not appeared. When they heard the news that the Santiago uprising had failed,

they realized they could wait no longer. Bitterly disappointed, they returned to their homes.

Shipwrecked on Cuba

The *Granma* finally reached Cuba at dawn on Sunday, but not quite as Castro had expected. Thanks to bad navigation, they were 1 mile (1.5 km) from the beach where they had planned to land. Instead of beaching the ship and leaping onto the sand, they ran aground on a mud-bank hundreds of yards from the shore. To reach dry land, they had to jump in the water and wade ashore with whatever equipment they could carry. "This wasn't a landing, it was a shipwreck!" was how Castro remembered their return to Cuban soil.

Worse was to come. A mangrove swamp lined the shore. Castro's force had to fight their way through a jungle of leaves and clamber over barriers of roots. None of them was really fit for the ordeal: their ship had carried only enough supplies for five days. After a week on board, all of them were tired, hungry, and thirsty.

The landing took two hours. When the rebels had regrouped, they set off inland.

The first Cuban they met was Pérez Rosabal, a simple charcoal maker. Castro hailed him grandly: "Have no fear. I am Fidel Castro. We have come to liberate the Cuban people!" As Rosabal shared what little food he had with a handful of ravenous rebels, explosions ripped across the coast. Castro's landing had not been as secret as he had hoped, and the Cuban airforce was bombing the mangrove swamp.

▼ *The map below shows some main towns and cities in Cuba and some of the places mentioned in this book.*

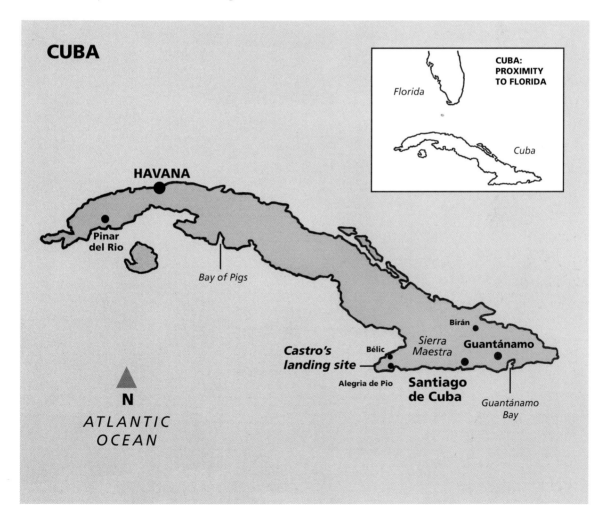

The rebels head for the hills

Afraid that the shelling would spread inland, Castro ordered his resting men to their feet. The rebels headed for the safety of the Sierra Maestra—Cuba's rocky, mountainous spine. This wild area was almost deserted. When rain fell, it would turn the mountain roads to mud, putting the revolutionaries' camp beyond reach of a ground attack. To Castro and his men, the mountains were a safe haven. Reaching them though, meant a long march through difficult country.

Fortunately for the rebels, most of the peasants they met were sympathetic to the revolutionary cause. The rebels received shelter, food, and drink, and were guided on their way. Nevertheless, it was a grueling march, and the weary rebels were still very hungry. To sustain themselves, they cut and chewed sugar cane. Experienced soldiers would have known to collect the chewed stalks, but Castro's men were raw recruits. They dropped the stalks where they finished them, leaving a record of their route as clear as any map. By the fourth day, the rebels could walk no farther. As night fell, they flopped down on a low hill above a cane field at Alegría de Pío.

At 4:30 the next morning, the sound of gunfire jolted them awake. Batista's spies had directed the army to the general location of Castro's forces. The trail of cane led them straight to the rebel camp.

Unprepared, groggy from sleep, and mostly barefoot, Castro's men made easy targets. Three were killed on the spot; 40 were captured, and either executed or imprisoned; 20 just disappeared.

▶ *The failure of the first attempt at revolution forced Fidel and the other survivors to take to the hills where they trained themselves in guerrilla warfare.*

¡Viva la Revolución!

When the attack at Alegría de Pío scattered the rebel force, Castro fled into a cane field with a pair of his comrades. "I was commander-in-chief of myself and two others," he later joked, but at the time he wasn't laughing.

After five days hiding in the cane field, Castro and his companions decided it was safe to move. In fact, they *had* to move, safe or not. They were gasping with thirst, and starving. They crept warily from the field, and when they were sure that the army was no longer searching for them, they struck out for the mountains.

Just a minor setback

Castro was as usual supremely confident. For him the cane field attack was not a defeat, it was simply the first battle of the revolution. His optimism gave the other two men strength, but it was hard going. They pushed on, and after two nights of walking reached the shack of a sympathetic coffee farmer. He sheltered the three men, fed them, then led them further into the hills, to the home of a member of the July 26th Movement.

Before long, more rebels who had fled the ambush joined them, swelling the guerrilla army from three to twenty. Castro was delighted to find that among the reinforcements were his brother Raúl and Che Guevara. Che had been shot in the shoulder, and though his wound was painful, it was not serious enough to require hospital treatment.

The rebels realized that the mountains offered them security they could not find anywhere else on the island. If they could reach the highest peaks, they could easily beat off Batista's army attacks. So they pressed on. Their march to the mountains eventually became a way of life, because in the following months they never stayed in one place for more than a few nights. Constantly moving from camp to camp kept them safe.

▶ *Initially forced into the mountains for their own safety, Castro's rebel soldiers became skilled in guerrilla warfare.*

38

First ambush

Though their numbers were increasing steadily, they still had few weapons. To get more, Castro decided in mid-January to attack an army post. He chose a small guard-post on the coast. The ragged rebel army moved into positions above the post. For two days they just watched and prepared for action. They launched their attack in the early hours of the morning, and when the soldiers refused to surrender, Che Guevara and another rebel set fire to the wooden barracks, driving out the soldiers. In this, their first real military action, the guerrillas captured nine rifles, a submachine gun, ammunition, food, and medicine.

Later, similar raids on small, badly defended military posts would win them more guns and bullets. Supporters in the lowlands helped supply them, too: one rebel woman climbed to their mountain camp with nine sticks of dynamite and 300 machine-gun bullets hidden under her skirt!

However, it was the resourceful peasants of the Sierra Maestra who were usually the rebels' guardians, guides,

◀ *A rare photograph showing a rebel making bombs at a secret location.*

messengers, allies, and recruits. The peasants were used to hardship and hunger; they knew every rock on every mountain; most hated the Batista dictatorship, and sympathized with Castro's aims. They kept the rebels supplied with food, and led them to the safest places where they could not be found.

Betrayed to the enemy

Not *all* of the peasants were loyal to the rebel cause, though. One peasant betrayed their hideout to the army, and the rebels came close to losing everything they had gained. At the end of January the informer guided military aircraft to Castro's mountain camp. One bomb scored a direct hit on the stove where breakfast was cooking. Fortunately there were no casualties, and the incident taught the rebels a valuable lesson: they became twice as cautious of traitors.

About two weeks after the attack, Castro met a woman who was to become his closest companion for nearly a quarter of a century. Celia Sanchez had been an important member of the rebel movement since the Moncada attack. She had sent food to Castro and his comrades in jail; it was Celia who got hold of the charts (sea maps) of the coast of Cuba where the *Granma* came ashore. But until February 1957, she had never seen the organization's leader face-to-face.

The two were powerfully attracted to each other, and though her work took her away from Castro at first, in the autumn she returned to the Sierra Maestra to share the rugged life of the rebels. She was his trusted friend, reliable secretary, and careful housekeeper. As another rebel remembers: "Celia never left him; Celia was always with him."

The rebels' strength grew throughout 1957. By July there were 200 rebels hiding in the mountains, and they had begun to take control of some of the more remote regions. By the following year, they were ready to expand rebel territory further north. Castro's brother Raúl commanded the advancing force of guerrillas. To exaggerate their strength, Raúl's group was named "Column No. 6," even though columns 2, 3, 4, and 5 never existed.

While Castro was training his warriors in the mountains, he did not neglect propaganda, spreading news and rumors in support of the revolution. He knew he had to persuade *all* the people of Cuba that he could beat the Batista regime. He set up a radio station, *Radio Rebelde*, on a mountain-top, beaming exciting stories to the island. He also gave interviews to newspaper and TV reporters.

A hero in New York

When an American writer visited the mountain hideaway, Castro ordered his men to march up and down constantly outside. He also pretended that the camp was just a small outpost, and that there were many much bigger camps elsewhere in the mountains. The reporter was taken in, and his article in the *New York Times* made Castro look like an unbeatable hero.

This horrified Batista, and he ordered the *Times* censored before it was put on sale in Cuba. Clerks obediently snipped the articles from the front pages, but a few copies slipped through the net. Sympathizers in the U.S. also reprinted the articles, and secretly shipped them to Cuba.

▶ *Wearing his July 26th Movement armband, Castro interrogates a prisoner at one of the rebels' strongholds.*

Circulated hand to hand, the articles transformed Castro's image. Before he had looked like a dreamer with a few loyal, but half-crazy, hangers-on. Batista had even claimed Castro was dead. But the *New York Times* built Castro up into a real guerrilla leader, suggesting for the first time that the day might soon come when he ruled Cuba.

Castro was not the only one scheming to destroy the dictator—there were many other rival organizations. In March 1957 student revolutionaries had stormed the presidential palace and Batista only narrowly escaped assassination. Two months later another former president of Cuba paid for an invasion very similar to Castro's, but the army rounded up and shot most of those who took part. Cuba's Communist Party also wanted to grab power and saw Castro as an obstacle, not an ally.

Castro schemes for power

Even within the July 26th Movement, not everyone recognized Castro's

◀ Another photograph of Castro interrogating a prisoner at a mountain hideaway; he appears fierce despite the over-sized glasses.

authority. The struggle for power and leadership reached a climax when the Movement organized a general strike on Easter in 1958. Radio messages called on everyone to stop work, go into the streets, and protest. The strike was a flop. By blaming the Movement's organizers in the cities and lowlands for the failure, Castro managed to undermine and eliminate his rivals.

By the summer of 1958, Batista realized he could not cling on to power unless he crushed Castro's rebels. So the dictator's generals planned a major attack. Ten thousand troops would surround the Sierra Maestra and gradually advance to encircle the rebels. Aircraft and battleships offshore would attack the rebel bases.

Castro had only 300 guerrillas; each of them had fewer than 50 bullets. It seemed like an unequal battle, but Castro was becoming used to unequal battles. The rebels may have been few in number, but each one of them was determined to win. Thanks to their wanderings over the Sierra Maestra hills, they were familiar with every peak and valley. Government troops could not have been more different: many were conscripts—they were being forced to fight—and they had never before left Cuba's towns and lowlands.

Fidel is finished?

The campaign was optimistically code-named "FF" for *Fin de Fidel* (The End of Fidel). It began around May 20, and at first, Batista forces made rapid progress. Cuban government aircraft pounded the rebel bases, killing and wounding many fighters. The planes were refueling and reloading with bombs at the United States base at Guantánamo. Raúl Castro was furious that the U.S. was helping the dictator in this way, so he took 49 American hostages—marines, and mining and sugar-plant workers. This trick ended the air campaign. Batista knew that if a bomb killed a hostage, he would lose U.S. support.

As the campaign dragged on, it turned in the rebels' favor. On the ground the conscript soldiers were no match for Castro's dedicated volunteer fighters, who showered bullets from mountain peaks they held. As the summer ended, so too did the battles. With the army retreating, Castro's rebels could afford to celebrate. They had taken hundreds of weapons

Why is there a U.S. base on Cuba?

Guantánamo Bay at Cuba's south-eastern end is one of the world's largest natural harbors. At the end of the 1800s, the United States recognized the importance of the bay and built a military base there. From it they could control the Windward Passage, the 50-mile (80-kilometer) wide strait between Cuba and Hispaniola that is the main shipping route to the Panama Canal.

When the U.S. handed Cuba back to its people in 1902, they kept the base, and have operated it ever since, in spite of many requests from Castro that U.S. troops leave the island. In 2002 the base was used as a jail for Al Qaida prisoners of war captured by American troops in Afghanistan.

from prisoners, and had even captured two tanks.

For Batista, it was the beginning of the end. Support for Castro had been growing rapidly right across the country as *Radio Rebelde* reported stories of government retreats and setbacks.

▶ *As the revolution progressed, Castro's army became better armed. Here, rebels with a machine gun keep watch over a road leading to Havana shortly before the victory over the Batista regime.*

Fighting back against Batista

By mid-August Castro's fighters had had time to recover from the summer attacks. They were fit and eager to make the final push against the dictatorship. Che led a group to a province east of Havana, another group moved into position west of the capital, and a third advanced on Santiago. Castro himself stayed in the mountains until November, then led his troops towards Guisa. Capturing this small town, some 30 miles (50 kilometers) away, would give the rebels control of a crucial road.

But the soldiers defending Guisa did not give up the town easily. They fought off Castro's attack, and the Cuban airforce supported them, bombing rebel troops around the town. After ten days' fighting, though, the defenders realized that no further troops were coming to help them, and they retreated to the west. Rebel fighters cautiously moved in, capturing more weapons—a tank, mortars, and bazookas. Cheered by the victory, Castro advanced along the road

◀ *January 8, 1959—Fidelito, Castro's son, is shown standing on a tank gun, on the day his father marched triumphantly into Havana.*

to Santiago. By Christmas he was a day's march from the provincial capital.

The dictator flees

Meanwhile, at his estate outside Havana, Batista realized he did not have much time left. There was open opposition to his government both in Havana and in the countryside, and he could no longer rely on his soldiers and airmen. At the stroke of midnight on New Year's Eve, he resigned. Two hours later he flew to safety in the Dominican Republic. Castro had won!

Freedom Fighter to Politician

"For the first time the republic will really be entirely free. . . . The people will have what they deserve. This war has been won by the people!"

The Santiago crowd cheered wildly at Castro's first speech as Cuba's leader. However, he did not pretend that the future would be easy. Although the war was over, he warned them, the revolution had only just begun, ". . . and the revolution will be a very difficult undertaking, full of danger."

But even Castro could not have known how many difficulties and dangers the future would bring. There was a hint of the troubles to come almost as soon as Batista fled. The United States saw Castro as dangerous and unpredictable, and backed senior army officers when they tried to form a junta—a military government. When he learned of the plan, Castro was defiant, announcing over *Radio Rebelde* that the Americans would NOT take over Cuba as they had in 1898 (see p. 6).

The junta collapsed in less than a day; it couldn't compete with Castro's hugely popular rebel movement. When Castro's troops began arriving in Havana around noon on January 2, 1959, they were cheered as heroes. Castro did not reach the capital for another six days— he traveled all the way from Santiago in an open-topped jeep, and stopped many times to make unplanned speeches. Just outside Havana he stopped one final time, to be reunited with his son, Fidelito, whom he had not seen since leaving Mexico.

When Castro at last entered the Cuban capital, the black and red banners of the July 26th Movement were everywhere, and the streets roared with cries of

▶ *When Castro reached Havana, jubilant crowds waving flags greeted him.*

51

"¡**VIVA FIDEL!**" (LONG LIVE FIDEL!).

Hanging up the rifles

It should have been a moment of triumph, but Castro did not share the hysterical happiness of the crowds. After years of guerrilla warfare in the mountains, the packed streets of Havana came as a shock. He had been a soldier, a rebel, and a guerrilla. Now he had to become a politician, a statesman, and a diplomat. It was not an easy change.

Of course, Castro had prepared for the responsibility of government. Many months before his triumphant entry into Havana, he had even chosen a president, Manuel Urrutia. This well-respected judge was a liberal, he favored freedom and democracy, and did not cling strongly to traditional ideas. At the time Urrutia seemed like a sensible choice. His moderate views meant he would be accepted by both sides—not only by the rebels, but also by those who did not trust Castro himself.

Urrutia lost no time. He quickly formed a cabinet—a small committee to govern the country. He chose as its members respected Cubans who had refused to be corrupted when Batista was in power. As prime minister, he named José Miró Cardona, a lawyer and one of Castro's teachers from the university.

Cuba's two presidents

The Cabinet set to work on Cuba's many urgent problems. They began to restore Cubans' human rights, and they fired officials who had helped and supported the dictatorship. Increasingly though, Urrutia discovered that Cuba actually had two presidents. He was the official president, ruling from the presidential palace, but real power lay with Castro, ruling from a suite on the top floor of the Hilton Hotel.

Urrutia got on with the exhausting business of governing the country. Castro made speeches, Castro appeared on TV, Castro gave newspaper interviews, Castro was the public face of the Cuban revolution. More and more, Castro used his speeches and interviews to announce grand plans for "his" nation. Often, they were the exact opposite of plans made by the cabinet, and announced by Urrutia. It couldn't last, and after less than two

◀ *Castro makes a political point during his first speech after he had been sworn in as prime minister of Cuba, February 16, 1959.*

months in office, Miró Cardona resigned. Fidel Castro took complete control.

Though he was in charge of the country, Castro found it difficult to adapt to the role of politician. He was used to action, not endless discussion of policy details. His government faced constant criticism, especially for the execution of Batista's henchmen, the police and soldiers who had tortured and murdered at the dictator's command. Those who could not escape from the island when Castro came to power were quickly rounded up and put on trial for their crimes. Many were executed; the rest got long prison sentences. When foreigners attacked Castro for the executions, he became angry. He pointed out that nobody had criticized Batista when his henchmen assassinated the dictator's opponents.

Criticism of the trials and executions reached fever pitch in April 1959 when Castro visited the United States, Canada, and several South American countries. In the United States news reporters quizzed him not only about the executions, but also about whether he was a communist. Americans feared the power of communist nations, especially

What is communism?

Under a communist political system, a nation's people, or its government, own and control all land, farms, factories, and houses. Private property and individuality are discouraged. Everyone is supposed to receive everything they need from the government.

Communism is the direct opposite of the U.S. political system, which believes in democracy and individual freedoms. Government control of business under communism contrasts with the capitalist system operating in the United States under which factories and farms are privately owned and people are encouraged to get rich by working hard.

Until the end of the 20th century, communism was the system of government used in the Soviet Union (now Russia and many smaller countries), in Eastern Europe, and in North Korea, Vietnam, and China.

the Soviet Union. The Soviets feared the U.S. equally, and these two "superpowers" had each armed themselves with powerful nuclear weapons in case the other attacked. The tense rivalry of the time was known as the Cold War.

▶ *Shown are Castro (right) and the liberal judge Manuel Urrutia, the first president of post-revolutionary Cuba.*

"I am not a communist"

Castro replied to questions about communism by claiming over and over again that he was not a communist. The few communists in his government had little power, he said. He reassured American businessmen that no Cuban government would steal their land or property in Cuba. But he also admitted that there would be no free elections for at least four years because, "real democracy is not possible for hungry people."

Castro tried hard to make his visit to the United States a success. He swapped his baggy, grubby, olive-green combat suit for a neatly tailored and pressed olive-green combat outfit. He controlled his quick temper and tried to be patient and polite. His appearances drew huge crowds, but he returned to Cuba without the trade deals he had been hoping for.

Back home again, Castro returned to some of the promises he had made to the Cuban peasants. He passed a new land law which limited the size of privately-owned farms to 5.3 square miles (1,375 hectares), a plot of land small enough to cover by foot. It was a popular move among Cuba's landless peasants, but the law threatened big landowners. They were not Castro's only critics. The country's president, Manuel Urrutia, accused Castro of drifting towards communism. Castro was not prepared to allow criticism from his own ministers, so he forced Urrutia to resign.

Castro had guessed that the new land law would be unpopular in the United States. U.S. companies owned huge farms in Cuba, some of them 500 times bigger than the new limit. Castro guessed right. The changes he was making in Cuba dismayed and worried the U.S. government. It worried U.S. businessmen more. U.S. investment in Cuba dried up.

◀ *During his visit to Washington in 1959, Castro abandoned his usual combat gear for a military-style uniform*

Cuba Goes Red

From Moscow, the capital city of the Soviet Union, Cuba looked like a very small blob on a very big map. When news that Castro had kicked out the Cuban dictator reached the Kremlin, where the Soviet government met, it barely caused a stir. After all, why should the Soviets be interested in Castro?

On the face of it, he didn't seem like an ally. As a student he had had little to do with Cuba's official Communist Party. As a revolutionary Castro never suggested he wanted to make Cuba into a communist nation. When he first came to power, the changes he made had more to do with freedom and social justice than with communism. Gradually, though, all this began to change. As the U.S. government became more and more unfriendly to Cuba, the Soviet government grew more helpful.

The sweet smell of aid

It started quietly, with sugar. Just seven weeks after Castro came to power, he offered to sell the Soviets some of Cuba's sugar crop. They bought half a million tons of the 1959 harvest.

The Cubans and Soviets did not meet officially for another year, when Soviet politicians flew to Havana to talk about trade— sugar, guns, sugar, oil, sugar, embassies, and sugar. Each country agreed to open an embassy (a government office) in the capital of the other, and Castro struck a deal to export a million tons of sugar a year to the Soviet Union. In exchange, Cubans would get technical assistance and a shopping list of things they desperately needed: fuel, wheat, iron, steel, aluminium, paper, and chemicals.

This new agreement between its greatest enemy and its nearest overseas neighbor alarmed the United States.

▶ *In this picture, wagons of sugar cane await processing at a factory outside Santiago. Castro wanted profits from sugar to help rebuild Cuba.*

Already cold towards Castro, U.S. politicians became openly hostile.

Cuban-American relations got even worse in March 1960, when a ship loaded with ammunition and explosives blew up in Havana harbor, killing 81 people. Without waiting for an investigation, Castro angrily accused the United States of sabotage. The American ambassador later described his behavior as ". . . insulting and aggressive . . . ."

Oil trouble

In the summer insults turned to actions. Thanks to the earlier deal with the Soviet Union, the Cubans were importing crude oil. To refine it (turn it into gasoline and other fuels), they nationalized three oil refineries on the island. The American and British owners received nothing.

The U.S. response, a week later, was to stop all sugar imports from Cuba. Castro called the move "the Dagger Law" because, he said, it stabbed the Cuban revolution in the back. Losing sugar sales to the United States would cause enormous hardship to Cubans, because sugar and cigars were practically the only things the country exported.

Again, it was the Soviets who came to the rescue. In Moscow, Nikita Krushchev, the Soviet premier, announced that his nation would buy all the sugar the United States had turned away. "The Soviet Union is extending a helping hand to the people of Cuba . . . ." he said. Then he continued, ". . . if it became necessary, the Soviet Union could support the Cuban people with rocket weapons." It was a clear warning to the United States to leave Cuba alone.

Castro's revenge

Meanwhile in Havana, Castro was plotting revenge and in August he struck. He nationalized almost all U.S. businesses on the island. Oil refineries, sugar mills, and cattle ranches worth $850 million instantly became the property of the Cuban nation. Two months later the Cubans took over two rich nickel mines. As before, their American owners were not paid anything.

Castro's drift towards communism did not end with control of industry. He became less tolerant of criticism in the

▶ *In September 1960 the growing relationship between the Soviet and Cuban leaders was captured by the world's journalists.*

press, and on TV and radio. Newspapers that published articles unfavorable to the government were made to print the official view in a paragraph at the end of each article. Eventually they were forced out of business.

The only newspapers that remained were obedient servants of the government. When the "Maximum Leader" visited New York in September 1960, his trip was reported without criticism in Havana. Officially Castro was in the United States to represent Cuba at the United Nations—the "club-of-all-countries" founded in 1945 to promote peace and trade. However, he had another reason for coming to New York. Nikita Krushchev was in town for the same UN meeting, and the two leaders met twice for friendly talks. Americans could only watch as the two enemies of their country hugged and laughed in the middle of Manhattan. It looked as though Castro was doing his best to insult his U.S. hosts.

Trade blockade

If he was, he succeeded. Soon after Castro returned to Cuba, the United States ambassador flew home from Havana. The next day, the United States banned all exports to Cuba except essential food and medicines. The separation between the two countries was complete.

The move towards communism was having effects at home, too. Discontent and rebellion simmered. Counter-revolutionary groups had formed in the Escambray Mountains in central Cuba, and in Oriente—Castro's home province in the east. Once a rebel himself, Castro had become an enemy of rebellion, fighting back against the small but growing number of Cubans who were taking up arms to oppose him.

There was unhappiness in the fields, too. Ownership of the sugar cane farms had changed, but life for the workers had not. In fact, if anything, the revolution made things worse. Unemployment had risen; wages fell by a fifth; working hours rose from eight to nine hours a day. Peasants who could afford to do so left the country. Many wealthy families had already left when Castro extended his program of nationalization to take control of their farms, banks, and businesses in

▶ As the UN meeting progressed in September 1960, the obvious friendliness of Castro and Krushchev began to alarm the U.S. government.

October 1960. Frightened by Castro's communist sympathies, middle-class people followed. Some of them were engineers, scientists, and doctors whose skills were vital to the welfare of the entire country.

In all, perhaps 250,000 of Cuba's six million people fled in the three years after Castro came to power. Castro did not seem to care. He called them "parasites" and said he was glad to see them go. In Cuba, they could cause trouble; in the U.S., he figured, they were harmless. But as he would soon find out, he was mistaken.

▶ *During a visit to the Soviet Union in January 1964 to build Cuban-Soviet relations, Castro tries out skiing.*

The Bay of Pigs

Almost as soon as Fidel Castro took power in Havana, American politicians started to discuss ways to get rid of him. When Castro began to turn his country into a communist nation, the discussions became more and more urgent.

Once Castro had formed alliances with the Soviet Union, the simplest approach—an invasion of Cuba by the United States—was out of the question. If U.S. troops were involved, Cuba's powerful communist ally would certainly defend the island.

So the CIA settled on a more subtle invasion plan. The invaders would not be Americans, but Cubans! Thousands of refugees had fled to the U.S. after the revolution, and many had settled in Florida. They hated Castro. With money and guns from the CIA, they could invade Cuba. Once ashore, opposition groups on the island would help them remove Castro from power.

Blame the Cubans

It was a daring plot. If it succeeded, the United States would have been rid of an irritating communist government uncomfortably close to home. Even if the plan failed, no American soldiers would be involved. The U.S. government could blame everything on Cuban counter-revolutionaries.

To minimize the risk, the CIA did everything they could to keep the plan secret and hide U.S. involvement. They built a training camp in Guatemala, far away from the United States. There the Cubans could get fit and learn to use weapons in complete secrecy. When everything was ready, fruit ships—rather than the U.S. navy—would carry the men across the Caribbean to Cuba.

Even the aircraft they planned to use in the attack would be flown by Cuban refugees and painted with Cuban airforce markings. If any of the pilots were caught, they could pretend to be *real* Cuban airmen who had stolen their aircraft to escape to the U.S.

▶ *Here, anti-Castro rebels train for action: their arms and ammunition were supplied by the CIA.*

The plan was so secret and sensitive that the CIA did not tell the rebel groups in Cuba the invasion date. Even America's new president, John F. Kennedy, learned of it only after he had won the election in 1960.

On Saturday April 15, 1961 the plan swung into action, starting with an air attack. Castro's tiny airforce posed a threat to the invasion craft, so six obsolete B26 bombers took off from Nicaragua and attacked the Cuban airstrips. The air attack destroyed some of Castro's planes on the ground, but crucially, eight were undamaged.

The counter-revolution begins

By the early hours of Monday morning, the fruit ships loaded with troops were off the Cuban coast, and the first landings began. The plan went wrong almost as soon as it had begun. Some of the landing craft struck rocks in the Bay of Pigs, the sheltered inlet chosen for the landing. The soldiers on board had to wade ashore. Though they succeeded in regrouping and setting up a base camp not far from the beach, Cuban militiamen (civilian part-time soldiers) spotted them,

opened fire, and raised the alarm.

Within an hour, the Cubans had launched a well-rehearsed defense plan. Castro had been expecting an invasion, and he ordered tanks and soldiers to rush to the Bay of Pigs. At the same time, the secret police rounded up members of opposition groups—35,000 in Havana alone. The rebels that the CIA were counting on for help were imprisoned before they knew about the invasion.

At the airfields inland, what was left of the Cuban air force sprung into action. Sea Fury fighters armed with rockets soared into the sky. Swooping low over the ocean, they spotted one of the invaders' ships and attacked with rockets. The crippled ship ran aground. When they attacked a second ship with machine-gun fire, it turned around and headed back out to sea. After refueling, the Sea Furies returned and sank another freighter carrying vital ammunition and supplies that the invading troops needed to push further inland. As the sun rose, the remaining ships turned and fled.

▶ *Cuban exiles are shown studying a map during their training for the Bay of Pigs invasion in April 1961.*

What is the CIA?

The United States's spy office is called the Central Intelligence Agency, or CIA. It was created in 1947 to collect and analyze information from all over the world that might be useful to U.S. leaders, and to prevent foreign spies from learning U.S. secrets.

The CIA sends agents all over the world. To protect them, the CIA must operate in complete secrecy. In the past the CIA has used this secrecy to hide its involvement in the attempted assassination of foreign leaders, including not only Fidel Castro, but also Patrice Lumumba, Prime Minister of the Democratic Republic of Congo. The CIA's "covert" (hidden) operations included the Bay of Pigs invasion and "Operation Phoenix." Twenty-thousand people died in this CIA-guided mission to catch communist agents in South Vietnam. By the 1980s the American public were becoming angry at the lack of control over the CIA, so in 1981 President Gerald Ford passed a law ending CIA murders abroad.

After the September 11, 2001 attacks on the United States, however, some Americans are saying that CIA spies must once again be allowed to use all necessary methods to prevent terrorism.

During the morning, the B26 bombers that had two days earlier attacked Cuba's airstrips returned. They were met by Cuban Air Force T-33 jet trainers. Most air forces used these small planes for teaching pilots before they graduated to real fighters. But the Cubans were short of cash so, unknown to the CIA, they had fitted out the T-33s with cannons. Fast and agile in flight, the T-33s attacked the lumbering bombers, downing four of them.

Castro may have won the air and sea battles, but the troops on land were not so easily defeated. The invaders held off the army and militiamen for two days, killing 161 of Castro's troops. When the invaders were finally defeated 1,200 of them were taken prisoner; more than 100 had died in the fighting.

Kennedy is humiliated

It was a humiliating defeat. CIA attempts to blame it on anti-Castro Cuban groups quickly fell apart. Far from being "deniable" as the agency had hoped, the attack had obviously been planned and aided by the U.S. In particular, the Kennedy administration was made to look foolish.

▶ *Once the scene of the failed anti-Castro invasion, the beach at the Bay of Pigs is now a popular tourist destination.*

▲ *Castro, in fighting spirit, leads his troops in an inspection of the beach where the anti-Castro forces had landed.*

▶ *Many of the prisoners taken at the Bay of Pigs fiasco were held as hostages. Here, some of them pose for the camera.*

When Castro and his police and soldiers quizzed the captured troops, the picture got even worse. Among the Cuban refugees recruited by the CIA were a dozen or so who had been assassins and torturers for the Batista government. These soldiers were put on trial, and some were executed for their earlier crimes. But most of the invaders were held as hostages. Castro offered to return them to the United States in exchange for 500 new tractors, which were badly needed in the Cuban fields. The U.S. government refused, and the captives remained in Cuba for a full year. It took until Christmas the following year to agree a deal, and the price of freedom was $53 million in food and medical aid.

The Bay of Pigs invasion confirmed Castro's view that the United States would do anything to remove him. And a year later his determination to defend himself against U.S. aggression was to bring the world to the brink of nuclear war.

Operation Mongoose

The CIA did not give up after the Bay of Pigs. They simply changed their approach. Instead of aiming for a revolution in Cuba, they decided to assassinate Castro.

At one point the CIA was employing 400 people to work on the plan. It was nicknamed "Operation Mongoose," after the resourceful rat-like mammals that attack and kill poisonous snakes.

Some of the CIA's plans to kill Castro might have worked: they paid Mafia gangsters to shoot him, and they tried to poison his food. But some murder plots were so bizarre that they would seem unlikely even in a spy novel. They included supplying Castro with exploding cigars, dusting his shoes with poison when he put them out to be cleaned in a hotel corridor, giving him a wet-suit coated with nerve poison (Castro was a scuba-diver), and planting an explosive clam shell on the sea-bed where he swam.

In 1964 and 1965 alone, the CIA sent assassins to kill Castro 30 times. None succeeded, and in all, Castro has survived more than 6,000 attempts on his life.

The Missile Crisis

Sitting in his pyjamas in his favorite rocking chair, President John Kennedy frowned at the photographs spread out on his lap.

The photographs, taken from high-flying spy planes, showed a patchwork of Cuban fields. New roads crisscrossed the landscape, and it was easy to spot huge concrete buildings under construction. A CIA chief had rushed the pictures to the White House early on the morning of Tuesday October 16, 1962. He told Kennedy there was only one possible explanation, the Soviet Union was building missile launch sites in Cuba! Each missile had a nuclear warhead powerful enough to flatten a large city. Launched from Cuba, the rockets would take only a few minutes to reach their targets.

Kennedy was dismayed, but he could hardly have been surprised. U.S. spies had been warning for months that there was frantic building work going on in the Cuban fields. Cuban people arriving in Miami had told stories of convoys of military vehicles, of hundreds of Russian-speaking "advisers" swarming all over the island, and of top-secret bases where no Cubans were admitted.

But until that Tuesday morning, it was hard to believe that the Soviets could think they could get away with such a bold insult to the United States—or that Castro would be stupid enough to allow them to build the bases.

The view from Havana

Castro saw things differently. The Bay of Pigs invasion had confirmed his suspicion that the U.S. wanted to crush the Cuban revolution. Castro was sure that another, bigger attack was planned, so in the spring of 1962, he discussed with the Soviets how Cuba could defend itself against attack. In the summer Che Guevara and Castro's brother Raúl traveled to Moscow to make final arrangements. By the end of August, shipments of machinery, building

▶ *An atom bomb is tested in the Nevada Desert. The nuclear arms race that Cuba was drawn into created enormous political tension worldwide.*

equipment, troops and weapons began pouring into Cuban ports.

To Castro, the new missiles were a necessary defense against the United States. To Kennedy, they were a dangerous challenge. And to Soviet Premier Krushchev, they were just one more step in the "nuclear arms race." The Soviet Union and the United States had been playing this dangerous game for more than ten years. The rules were simple. The two superpowers were competing to build ever-bigger nuclear bombs, and to outwit each other's defenses. U.S. missiles were aimed at Soviet cities and Soviet missile bases; Soviet missiles pointed the other way, threatening to destroy American cities and rocket launch sites.

The new bases on Cuba changed the rules. Previously all Soviet missiles had been situated in Russia or Eastern Europe, more than 7,000 miles (11,200 kilometers) away from the United States But now they were in America's backyard.

President Kennedy addresses journalists in April 1961, warning of the growing threat posed to the U.S. by an increasingly communist Cuba.

Kennedy called in his closest advisers. "We're going to take out these missiles," he told them, but he decided against immediate action. Instead, he asked the CIA to analyze how the Soviets would react to a U.S. attack on the missile sites. Meanwhile, the U.S. navy and air force were put on high alert.

Soviet lies

The next day, Kennedy met the Soviet Foreign Minister for two hours. The Russian politician assured the President that Soviet weapons in Cuba were purely for defense. Kennedy did not believe him. Two days later he decided to confront the Soviets.

Kennedy's challenge came in a short speech to the American people the following Monday. He demanded that the Soviet Union remove the missiles; he announced that the United States would surround Cuba with warships, and stop any further arms shipments; and he warned that if missiles were fired from Cuba, the United States would hit back by launching a nuclear attack—not on Cuba, but against the Soviet Union.

The reaction from Moscow was angry. The American president was, ". . . recklessly playing with fire. . . ," warned the Soviets, and he was risking nuclear war.

Castro was defiant, too. Vehemently he attacked "American aggression." The Cuban newspapers were censored, and did not at first reveal that there were Soviet missiles on the island. Nor did they mention details of Kennedy's speech.

The Cuban people, meanwhile, were calm. They knew what was going on by listening to foreign news broadcasts; but they had lived with the threat of U.S. invasions for so long that this seemed like just one more crisis.

The response from the rest of the world was one of sheer terror. The United States and the Soviet Union seemed to be teetering on the brink of a war that could—quite literally—destroy civilization.

▶ *This is an aerial photograph supposedly showing Soviet missile equipment on Cuban soil.*

▼ *Depicted is a tense moment as USS* Barry *turns a Soviet ship loaded with missile parts away from Cuba.*

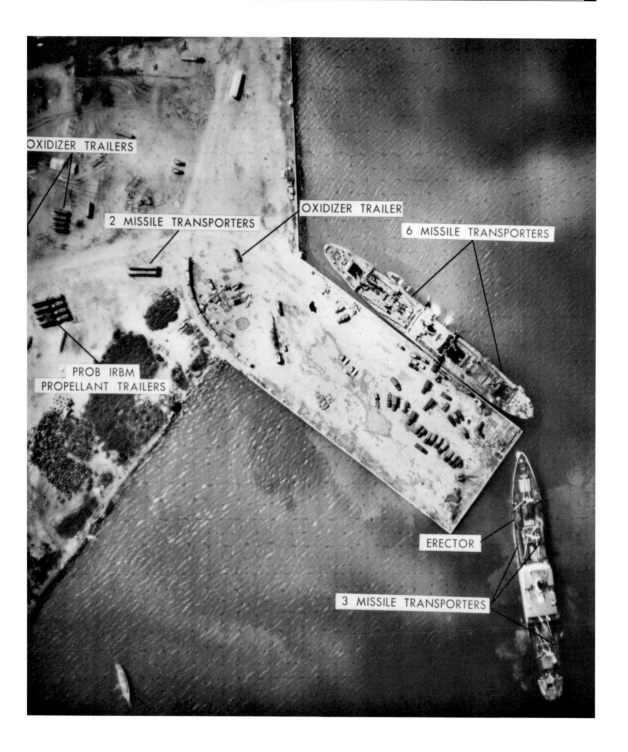

The world holds its breath

For a week the United States and the Soviets faced each other like two prize-fighters in a boxing ring, waiting to see who would make the next move. Behind the scenes, the two leaders exchanged angry messages. In meetings at the United Nations, Soviet and U.S. diplomats shouted each other down.

Soon though, it became clear that the Soviet leaders were weakening. Ships carrying more arms to Cuba did not challenge the U.S. naval blockade around the island. Krushchev made it clear that he did not want a nuclear war. By pointing out that there were U.S. bases on the Soviet Union's borders, in Greece and Turkey, he hinted at how the crisis might end.

On Friday a long letter arrived from Krushchev. In it he offered to remove the missiles from Cuba, in exchange for a promise that the United States would not invade the island. But even as the president was thinking about his reply, he received another message. In a broadcast over Moscow radio, the Soviets insisted that they would only do the deal if the United States also removed missiles from bases in Turkey.

A cunning solution

Kennedy asked his advisers what to do. After long discussions, they came up with a clever solution. They agreed that if the missiles were removed, the United States could withdraw its threat to invade Cuba. The second demand broadcast by radio was more of a problem. Agreeing to remove the missiles from Turkey would look like weakness. So although the president publicly ignored this request, he secretly promised to remove the missiles from Turkey at some time in the future. It worked. On Sunday, Moscow radio announced that the Soviets had accepted the U.S. peace offer. Around the world everyone heaved a sigh of relief.

▶ *On November 2, 1962, a relieved but serious President Kennedy addressed the country, assuring the American people that the Missile Crisis appeared to be over.*

Building a People's Paradise

Fidel Castro's revolution had promised Cuba's people land, freedom, and a better life. But delivering on these promises proved quite difficult.

Castro had grand plans for Cuba's factories and farms. The U.S. trade boycott was starving the island of essential factory-made goods, so he announced that Cuba would industrialize and become a manufacturing nation. Cubans would make everything they needed in many new factories. Castro was equally determined to make improvements in agriculture. Most land was planted with sugar cane, so Cuba had to buy a lot of food from foreign countries. Castro ordered farmers to rip out the cane and instead plant other food crops such as rice, beans, and peanuts.

The dream goes sour

Castro's vision of a new Cuba quickly ran into problems. Planning and management were poor, wasting money and scarce resources. New roads were made too wide,

so the tarmac ran out before the network was completed. Too many tractors were imported, but not enough plows and harrows. The best sugar cane fields were plowed up to make way for the new crops, but there was only enough seed to plant half of the fields. Fertilizer powder was left in the sun to bake into a useless lump, or was applied in dry weather when there was no rain to wash it into the soil. Castro himself interfered constantly, changing direction and making decisions that he should have left to others.

Not all of his decisions were the right ones. Assuming that every worker was filled with the same revolutionary enthusiasm as he was, Castro abolished bonus plans that rewarded hard work with higher pay. In factories production

▶ *Shown here are Cuban peasants hard at work in the sugar cane fields. Because of Castro's reforms the peasants owned and managed the fields.*

slumped, and the goods they produced were shoddy or faulty. This in turn led to shortages. With nothing to spend their money on, many people could see no reason to go to work.

The promise of freedom also turned sour, because in Castro's Cuba liberty was in short supply. Castro demanded that all arts should serve the revolution. Poets had to write revolutionary poems, artists had to paint revolutionary pictures, and musicians had to play revolutionary songs. These restrictions strangled the country's cultural life.

Stamping on liberty

Personal freedom was also restricted. Press censorship ended freedom of speech, and homosexuality was outlawed. Openly gay men were forced to join work gangs, alongside common criminals.

By 1963 it was clear that industrialization was failing, and Castro changed direction again. Farming would once more be the center of the country's economy. By concentrating on boosting sugar production, Castro hoped Cuba could earn the cash needed to make industrialization work.

He called this new program the "Ten Million Ton Harvest." In 1970 Castro announced that, farmers would grow, cut and process a record ten million tons of sugar. It was a bold and inspiring goal, and when it was announced, it looked possible: 1960 and 1961 had brought bumper harvests.

"Ten Million Ton Harvest"

However, over the next seven years, production did not rise as Castro had ordered. In fact it fell a little each year. The "Ten Million Ton Harvest" never happened. Despite the fact that Castro ordered everyone to cut cane—even children, old people, factory workers, and students had to help bring in the harvest —the 1970 crop weighed in at just 8.5 million tons. It was a record, but Castro's goal had just been too ambitious.

There was more bad news, too. The enormous effort that Cubans made to reach the target meant that they had neglected other industries. Not enough new cane seedlings had been planted to replace the old, worn out plants, leading to even smaller harvests in the following years. The sugar processing machinery, which had not been properly maintained, lacked vital spare parts and had been damaged in an effort to process the huge crop.

Castro did not hide the failure of his grand plan. Instead he tried to learn lessons from it. He took steps to improve planning and management in Cuba's factories and farms, and brought back money rewards for better and harder work. These changes produced some improvements—in 1972 alone, production increased by one fifth.

▶ *This 1960s Cuban poster features revolutionary heroes, including Che Guevara and Fidel Castro.*

The illusion of democracy

Castro also reformed Cuba's constitution (rules of government). He introduced democratic elections to local councils, and allowed these councils to choose representatives for the National Assembly (Cuba's parliament). However, these alterations did little to alter the *real* structure of government. The constitution, which was completed in 1976, made Fidel Castro leader for life. In effect, he was a dictator—a charismatic, inspiring dictator, it's true, but a dictator nonetheless.

Unfortunately you cannot eat charisma and inspiration, and many ordinary Cubans eventually lost faith in Castro's ability to improve their nation. Cuba's laws had made it difficult for them to leave the country, but in 1980 Castro announced that the rules would be lifted, so that anyone could emigrate. The flood of refugees that followed led Cubans to joke that they lived in the world's biggest country: the capital was in Havana, the government in Moscow, and the population lived in the United States.

◀ *Here, Castro poses for the camera to encourage everyone to take to the fields and bring in record harvests of sugar cane.*

The Mariel boat lift

In the early 1980s, Cubans desperate to escape the island began hijacking buses and driving them into the compounds of the Peruvian and Venezuelan embassies. When the embassies protected the fugitives, a furious Castro invited Cubans living in Florida to bring boats to the small port of Mariel to ferry would-be emigrants to the U.S. Big and small vessels, sometimes 600 a day, crossed the Straits of Florida and returned, often dangerously overloaded with passengers.

At first the U.S. government welcomed them, but as numbers grew, American immigration officials tried to stop the flood by arresting boat owners. In the end, more than 100,000 people fled from Mariel.

Making Friends Abroad

While Castro struggled to create the perfect communist state, he was not ignoring the world beyond Cuba's shores.

Almost as soon as he took power in Havana, Castro began trying to light the flame of revolution in neighboring countries. Castro's mission to spread communism caused enormous alarm in the United States. To understand why, think of world politics of the time as a board game.

Your move, Mr. President

There were just two players: the United States and the Soviet Union. They were competing to build an unbeatable shield of nuclear weapons. However, this Cold War game was not *just* about missiles. There was another, more stealthy way of winning—by capturing playing pieces from the board. The playing pieces were the world's less powerful countries. Under Cold War rules, the Soviet Union "captured" a piece from the board each time communists took power in a country. The American aim was the opposite—to fight communism everywhere, and to help governments that supported the United States.

"Capturing" Cuba was a great victory for the Soviet Union—and a defeat for the U.S. If one small nation in the Caribbean could turn communist, why not other larger nations elsewhere in Latin America (Central and South America and the Caribbean islands)?

Sowing the seeds of revolution

Fidel Castro was well aware of this possibility. So, as soon as his revolution succeeded, he began providing weapons, training, and support to Latin American

▶ *Krushchev and Castro shake hands on the 1964 deal for Cuba to supply the Soviet Union with thousands of tons of sugar.*

freedom fighters. In particular, he helped guerrillas in Chile and Venezuela.

In the Soviet Union, Castro's support for revolutionary movements was greeted with alarm. This may seem surprising, but to the Soviets, revolutions were dangerous things. The people who led them were unpredictable. Once they were in power, they had a nasty habit of going their own way and ignoring instructions from Moscow. The Soviet rulers had a different way of spreading communism. It didn't involve training guerrilla fighters and sending them arms and money. *They* preferred to support communist parties in nations where most of the people were unhappy with their rulers. Then, if the communists took power, the Soviet Union could control the new government.

Unwilling partners

This was what the Soviets hoped to do in Cuba. When Castro allowed the construction of missile bases on Cuba, it seemed as if the Soviets were getting their way. But the ending of the Missile Crisis (see p. 80) showed Castro that the Soviets did not really respect him. Removal of the missiles from the island made Castro furious. He felt they were a necessary defense against U.S. invasion. After this betrayal, Castro became an unwilling ally of the Soviets. He couldn't live without them, because he needed their aid and trade. But he didn't like being told what to do.

Increasingly, he looked for friends among the world's poorer nations. He found them in Africa, especially in African countries that had recently won independence from the European nations that had ruled them for a century or so. Cuba sent military aid, weapons, and medical supplies, and provided training, either in Cuba or in Africa. Castro's involvement in Africa caused anger in the United States. In 1969 U.S. officials warned that Cuban troops, then in sixteen African countries, were "a threat to permanent peace" on the continent.

African war— Cuban troops

Castro's strongest alliance was with revolutionaries who had waged a long and bitter struggle against the government of Portugal. This southern European nation ruled Mozambique,

▶ *Cuban soldiers in Angola were part of the military aid Castro sent to the MPLA.*

Angola, and Guinea Bissau. Cuban troops first went to Angola shortly after the country became independent. They helped the MPLA (Popular Movement for the Liberation of Angola) resist attacks by rival independence groups.

One of Castro's secret weapons in Africa was Che Guevara. In the spring of 1965, Castro's friend and ally had disappeared from Cuba, where he was supposed to be Minister for Industry. In fact, Castro's grip on Cuba was so tight that there was little for Che to do, and he had slipped out of the country to train Africans in guerrilla warfare. Che's mission took him to what is now the Democratic Republic of Congo (Kinshasa) and to Mozambique.

Adios Che

It's unclear how long Che Guevara spent in Africa, but we do know that at some point he left the continent and traveled to South America. On October 18, 1967, he was shot dead in the forests of Bolivia. He had gone there on a reckless mission

◀ *This Cuban poster celebrating Heroic Guerrilla Day emphasizes Che Guevara's involvement in South America.*

to help guerrillas who were fighting the country's government.

His friend's death shook the Cuban leader. Although Castro declared 1968 to be the "year of the heroic guerrilla" he began to give less help to foreign revolutionaries. The shock of Guevara's death was not the only reason for this: Cuba could simply not afford to give away as much aid; the government had almost run out of money. Cubans continued to fight in Africa, but Castro's attempts to spread a communist revolution in Latin America ended.

In time, Castro began to look for more peaceful ways to increase his influence in the developing world. He took a leading role in the Non-Aligned Movement. This club of around 100 poorer nations was formed in 1955 to resist domination and control by powerful, wealthier countries. In particular, members wanted to avoid alignment (alliances) with the Cold-War superpowers. Castro's involvement might seem surprising, because Cuba was firmly aligned with the Soviet Union. Though other members sometimes questioned his independence, Castro's influence grew. He became an important spokesman on issues such as aid to the developing world,

and the cancellation of debt—the money that poorer nations owed to rich nations.

Cuba's Peace Corps

Cuba also began exporting skills, sending engineers and doctors to deprived areas of the world. The country's universities and colleges welcomed students from these regions, training them in medicine and other aspects of science and technology. The medical program was the most successful of these plans and continues today, with more than 2,000 Cuban health workers in 15 countries. *The New York Times* compared Cuba's aid program to the U.S. program which sends volunteers to needy countries, calling Cuba's "the largest Peace Corps program of civil aid in the world."

All these steps made Castro an important figure in the world. But at home in Cuba, they did little to help the shortages and poverty caused by the nation's ruined economy. As the long-suffering Cuban people would discover, there was worse to come.

◀ *This is the last known photograph of Che Guevara. It was taken in Bolivia before his death in 1967.*

The Lone Red Flag

It should have been a glittering occasion of celebration. Soviet President, Mikhail Gorbachev, had come to Cuba in April 1989 to talk about friendship and cooperation. But even as he embraced the Soviet leader, Fidel Castro was deeply worried.

Cuba's old friend the Soviet Union was changing fast; Gorbachev was trying desperately to modernize his country. Under the policy of *perestroika* (restructuring) Gorbachev had already eliminated many government controls and opened up his country to private business. He had also given Soviet people more freedom. His *glasnost* (openness) formula allowed more free speech.

These changes were alarming enough for Castro, but they were tiny compared to the upheaval that would soon sweep Eastern Europe. By 1991 Gorbachev had lost control, and in the chaos that followed, the Soviet Union split apart.

The consequences for Cuba were disastrous. Two-thirds of Cuba's trade had been with the Soviet Union and other communist countries in Eastern Europe. By buying at least three million tons of sugar a year at four times the market price, the Soviets had propped up Cuba. The collapse of communism did not stop these countries trading with Cuba, but it changed how they did business. Now they wanted to pay market prices for Cuba's sugar. They also expected to be paid in American dollars for goods they *sold* to Cuba.

Rationing begins

There had been shortages of food and other essential goods in Cuba before Soviet support vanished. Now the Cuban people faced further hardships. Towards the end of 1990, rationing was extended to everything in the stores. Castro introduced a "special period in peacetime" rule to conserve energy and reduce public services. Despite calls for

▶ *At the start of Gorbachev's visit to Cuba, Castro and Gorbachev embraced. Castro was alarmed by Gorbachev's reforms of Soviet communism.*

reform, Castro was defiant. Rather than reduce government control, he vowed to extend it.

Despite this fighting talk, Castro was forced to make changes. In 1992 the law was altered to allow foreign companies to cooperate with Cuban businesses in joint projects. The following year, Cubans were permitted to save foreign money. Farmers were at last allowed to sell their surplus produce in markets.

These steps helped to reduce the Cuban government's debts. However, they spelled misery and hardship for the Cuban people. As poverty tightened its grip on the island, many more tried to escape to the United States (see box).

By 1994 though, Castro's changes began to have some effect. Each year that followed Cuba's people and government have had a little more money to spend.

Tourists to the rescue!

Much of Cuba's revenue now comes not from sugar, but from the tourists who flock to the island to soak up the sun. The Cuban government has built many

◀ *The old-world charm of unmodernized Cuba now brings in its main revenue, tourism dollars.*

Rafting to a new life

Ever since Castro's revolution, Cubans have tried to cross the narrow stretch of ocean that separates the island from the American mainland. The U.S. once welcomed them, but now returns to Cuba all those captured at sea.

Cuban refugees made headlines in 2000 when a six-year-old Cuban boy was rescued from the ocean. Elian Gonzalez's mother had drowned trying to cross with him. The boy's father wanted him back in Cuba, but relatives in Miami, Florida begged the government to let him stay with them.

After near-riots, the American courts decided to return Elian to his father.

new hotels and renovated others in Havana's historic streets. This, combined with some skilful marketing, tempts 160,000 Americans to defy their government's ban and travel to Cuba each year. Many more visitors come from Canada and Europe. All come to the island because it is so very different from every other country in the world. The difference between Cuba and its giant neighbor to the north is especially noticeable. Cuba is like a lonely red communist flag flapping brightly in the warm Caribbean air, and as long as Fidel Castro lives, it's likely to stay that way.

Hero or Monster?

Now in his seventies, Castro has a solid, if lonely, grip on power. He hears little criticism from the people he respects.

Raúl Castro, now head of Cuba's armed forces, seems unlikely to offend his brother. Castro's son, Fidelito, has little influence. His daughter Alina Revuelta, who fled to the United States in 1993, broadcasts anti-Castro messages from a Havana radio station, but hers is just one of many critical voices from abroad. The one person close to Castro who wasn't afraid to contradict him was his faithful companion Celia Sanchez, but she died in 1980.

Even those who dislike the Cuban leader admit that he is an extraordinary figure, an inspiring and persuasive character who gets ordinary people to do remarkable things. But what divides his admirers from his critics is what he has achieved for his country, and the way in which he did it.

It is very hard to look at Castro's life without bias. He turned Cuba into a communist country at a time when fear of communism was at an all-time high. In the United States in particular there is still bitterness about Castro's nationalization of American property and businesses.

Castro's supporters don't have a balanced view, either. They admire the way he led his revolutionary guerrillas to victory, but prefer to ignore the problems that followed.

But putting prejudice aside for a moment, what has Castro achieved in Cuba, and at what price?

One of his main priorities, from the moment he took power, was to improve Cuba's social services. By pouring money into medicine and education he ensured that Cubans lived longer, healthier lives, and that all children went to school. In 1959 four out of every ten Cubans could not read. Now almost everyone can.

Today Cuba's schools and hospitals are very short of money, yet health care and education are better than anywhere else in Latin America. If Cuban statistics

▶ *A portrait of Fidel Castro, taken in 1977. Most of his life he wore a distinctive beard and smoked cigars.*

are accurate (and not everyone agrees that they are) Cubans are healthier and better educated than people in many so-called developed nations.

On the other hand, Castro's management of his country's factories, farms, and businesses has, at times, been nothing short of disastrous. He alone must take the blame for the low standard of living, and for many of the shortages that make everyday life a constant struggle in the country.

In the wider world, his alliance with the Soviet Union briefly threatened the world with nuclear war. The "freedom fighters" that Cuba trained and equipped have been described as "terrorists" by the politicians they fought against in Latin America and Africa.

Cuba has a terrible record on human rights. Castro does not tolerate opposition of any sort, so there is no freedom of speech. His armed security forces are almost as ruthless at crushing opposition as the secret police of the dictatorship he fought so hard to destroy. Even peaceful protest is forbidden by law.

◀ *In September 1997 Castro gave a fighting speech to show that he was alive, despite rumors to the contrary.*

Anti-government newspapers and radio or TV stations simply do not exist in Cuba, and the country's jails are crowded with Castro's opponents. Some have been tortured or starved for their views.

The conditions in Cuba have driven hundreds of thousands of people to flee to the United States. A few were so desperate to escape that they tried to cross the ocean to Florida in dangerously overcrowded boats, or even in rubber rings.

Fidel Castro has of course become used to such criticisms. He has a great memory for figures, and fights back against attack with a barrage of statistics. However, there are few reasonable responses to the worst criticisms of the Castro regime.

Castro's bad management is not the only reason for the country's poverty. The blockade that the United States imposed on Cuba has—as intended—made trade extremely difficult for the country. When he is accused of sponsoring terrorism, Castro can point out that he condemned the September 11, 2001 attack on the World Trade Center. He is also fond of saying that the United States has funded terror abroad. Since 1946, the U.S. army has run the School of the Americas, which secretly trained soldiers in assassination. Graduates of the school have been involved in every major coup in Latin America.

Cuba's human rights record is almost impossible to defend. Castro's supporters reassure critics that some Latin American countries have a far worse human rights record than Cuba. This was briefly true in the 1980s, but independent human rights monitors suggest that, in fact, Cubans today have fewer freedoms than almost any other people.

On the subject of refugees, Castro's defenders point out that revolutions always drive away the people who oppose them. After the American Revolution, for example, between 50,000 and 100,000 Tories (British loyalists) left the United States—when the country had a population of only 2.5 million.

So is Fidel Castro a hero or a monster? Like most people he is probably neither. Political turmoil can bring out the best and the worst in people. Whatever you think of Castro, his impact on Cuba, and the world, cannot be denied.

▶ *Castro continues to rule Cuba with an iron grip, regardless of world opinion.*

Glossary

Ally Friend or supporter.

Ammunition Bullets or shells fired by guns.

Assassination The murder of an important person for political reasons.

Blockade Surrounding a city or country to stop supplies moving in or out.

Boycott Organized campaign to force change by refusing to trade with a nation.

Bribe Illegal and secret payment to obtain a favor.

Candidate Someone who seeks power by running for office.

Censor To stop news spreading by controlling broadcasters and publishers.

Civil Not military.

Column Group of army troops or vehicles.

Communism Political system in which property is owned by all, and everyone works for the benefit of the whole community.

Convict To prove that someone carried out a crime.

Corrupt Dishonest, willing to take *bribes*.

Democracy Form of government where decisions are made by everyone, or by people they have chosen in an election.

Dictator Ruler with complete power.

Dictatorship Country run by a *dictator*.

Economy Business and trade of a country.

Election Choice of a leader by voting

Export To send goods to another country.

Freedom of speech Freedom to criticize anything—even a country's rulers.

Guerrillas Soldiers who fight in small groups with the help of local people, relying on surprise attacks.

Hispaniola Island to Cuba's east, divided into Haiti and the Dominican Republic.

Hostage Prisoner who is released in exchange for money or special favors.

Human rights Basic rights and freedoms that all people deserve.

Idealistic Unrealistic or not practical.

Invasion Forced entry.

Investment Spending money on a project in the hope of making more.

Market price Price that goods are sold at when traded freely.

Minister The name for a senior politician in the governments of some countries.

Missile Rocket weapon.

Further reading

Nationalize To take a business under government control.

Parasite Animal, such as a flea, that lives on another animal.

Pardon To forgive.

Premier The top leader in some countries.

Racial prejudice Bad treatment of people because of their race.

Rebel Someone who uses force to oppose a government.

Rebellion Organized resistance to a government.

Recruit New member of an organization.

Revolution Sudden overthrow of one government and its replacement with another.

Revolutionary Suggesting revolution – or a person who organizes revolution.

Sabotage Damaging property to harm an enemy.

Slave Person bought and sold like property who must work for their owner.

Suicidal Knowingly risking death.

Terrorism Use of terror to gain political power.

Tory American who chose the British side in the American Revolution.

Ancona, George. *Cuban Kids*. New York: Cavendish Children's Books, 2000.

Bernard, Wolf. *Cuba: After the Revolution*. New York: Penguin Putnam Books for Young Readers, 1999.

Gibb, Tom. *Fidel Castro: Leader of Cuba's Revolution*. Austin, TX: Raintree Publishers, 2001.

Guevera, Ernesto. *Episodes of the Cuban Revolutionary War, 1956-1958*. New York: Pathfinder Press, 1996.

Keen, Benjamin. *A History of Latin America*. New York: Houghton Mifflin, 2000.

Timeline

1926 or 1927 Fidel Castro born near Birán, Oriente province, Cuba.

1945 Castro begins law school at Havana University.

1947 Castro joins a failed attempt to invade the Dominican Republic.

1948 Castro marries Mirta Díaz-Balart. April: as a student activist he takes part in riots in Bogotá, Colombia.

1949 Mirta gives birth to Castro's son.

1950 Castro graduates from the university and starts to work as a lawyer.

1951-2 Castro campaigns for election as an Orthodoxo party candidate in Cuba's House of Representatives.

1952 March 10: Fulgencio Batista takes control of Cuba in a *coup*.

1953 July 26: Castro jailed after a disastrous attack on Santiago's Moncada Barracks.

1955 May: Batista pardons political prisoners; Castro is released from jail.

Fall: Castro flees to Mexico and makes a fund-raising tour of the U.S.

1956 November 25: 81 rebels sail for Cuba in motor yacht *Granma*. The invasion is quickly detected, and most of the rebels killed or captured.

1957 Castro hides out in Cuba's *Sierra Maestra* mountains, rebuilding the strength of his guerrilla army.

February: Castro meets and falls in love with Celia Sanchez.

1958 Easter: following the failure of a planned nationwide strike, Castro takes control of the rebel movement.

May: Batista launches a major attack on the rebels. The rebels fight back, winning control of the country.

1959 January: Batista flees and Castro becomes the Cuban leader.

July: Cuba's President, Manuel Urrutia, is forced to quit; Castro's power grows.

1960 Castro loses U.S. support by nationalizing U.S. farms and businesses, and by striking a trade agreement with the Soviet Union.

September: Castro visits New York.

1961 April: an army of Cuban exiles, trained and equipped by the CIA, try unsuccessfully to invade Cuba at the Bay of Pigs.

1962 October: the discovery that Soviet missiles are based in Cuba leads to a crisis that threatens the world with nuclear war.

1967 Che Guevara shot in Bolivia.

1970 Castro's "Ten Million Ton" sugar harvest falls short of its target.

1975 Castro sends the first Cuban troops to fight in Africa.

1976 Following the introduction of a new constitution, Castro gives up the role of premier, and instead becomes president of the Council of State and Council of Ministers.

1979 Castro becomes president of the movement of non-aligned nations.

1980 Thousands of Cubans flee to the U.S. in small boats from Mariel port.

1990 Soviet aid to Cuba is reduced, forcing Castro to make further cuts in the standard of living of Cuban people.

1991 The Soviet Union collapses, triggering economic crisis in Cuba.

1992 Castro is forced to abandon some of his most extreme communist policies; the Cuban economy begins to slowly grow.

1994 After anti-government demonstrations in Havana, Castro ends ban on emigration.

2002 U.S./Cuban relations grow more friendly after Castro offers help in the imprisonment of terrorist suspects at Guantánamo Bay military base.

Index

References shown in italics are pictures or maps.